Dedication:

Volume 2 Assembly:
A Social Practice Get-Together
Sleepover Participants
2014

The Dedication Project

Visit The Dedication Project website at: www.dedicationproject.com.

First Printing June 2014.
Createspace: An Amazon Company

Title ID: 4863608
ISBN-13: 978-1500245634

1

Dedication:

Volume 2 Assembly:
A Social Practice Get-Together
Sleepover Participants
2014

The Dedication Project

Authors:
Eric John Olson || Shawna Vacca || JAH Justice ||
Samantha Loven || Nadine F. Edwards || Epiphany
Couch || Ethan Furniss || Roz Crews || Amanda Evans ||
S. Schumacher || Cris Scorza || Zachary Gough ||
Gemma-Rose Turnbull

Created by: Arianna Warner

For Jessica.

Without your love and strength I would not be able to continue pushing myself to explore my own boundaries. Without you, my sister and friend, I couldn't take the risk to fail. Without you, I wouldn't have been able to survive out childhood. To you I wish the void that created the possibility of the expanding universe.

For Hank Mycko.

For almost single-handedly giving me my mojo back.

For Michael Karl Ritchie.

For teaching me that you're never too old to be strange, dedicating countless hours to indoctrinating me into the media landscape of a counter culture, being the first person ever to put a microphone in my hand, and for being the first person to believe that I had something important to say.

For my Family.

Thank you for being such a part of me. For nourishing me and giving me all of your love, time, and care. I dedicate this writing and this moment to you. Thank you.

For my Mother.

You have given me love and acceptance throughout the past twenty-five years. Your hard work has taught me strength, motivation, and responsibility. I will always remember the times you've made me smile and laugh. You are devoted, selfless, and wise. I am so proud to call you Mom.

For Linda Couch.

You have taught me that compassion is invincible, and a life filled with compassion is a rich one. Thank you.

For Jeffery Steven Furniss.

You have been the most impactful person in my life. His strong personality has been that of a parent, life coach, mentor, mind trainer, and idea imposer. Without his constant babbling and critique of the world around us, my creativity and outlook would not be what it is today.

For Uzi Baram and Kim Anderson.

You continue to inspire me each time we talk.

For Loren Baker.

My teacher and mentor who taught me to make time for other people, no matter how busy I am. This November Loren died unexpectedly, and as it is so often with death, we didn't realize how much we loved and needed him until we experienced the gaping hole of his loss. I hope to someday become the incredible supporter, mentor, and teacher he was for me and countless others.

For whoever designed this carpet I'm sitting on as I write this.

Because no one ever dedicates anything to the people who design carpet.

For Valeria.

Your humble nature, ethics, and commitment to the work that you do and to bettering the world for all is admirable. I dedicate my practice to you every time I have a conversation with a work of art and people to dialogue with about their context and how artists are agitators that pose questions about our social responsibility; I think about you and all you help people.

For my oldest Brother, Jason.

Your consistent love and support reaches around the world.

For my darling Nan.

I tell people about you all the time. I brag about how I come from a family of really clever, wonderful, strong women. I tell them about how progressive and intellectually engaged you are-- how you have never stopped learning and being curious about the world. I really admire the way you think about things (and such diverse things) so clearly and non-judgmentally. I also tell people how comforting you are-- how you always gave me the best hugs when I was tiny, (your hugs are still great!), and how you soothed me if I was sad. Sometimes when I feel overheated and frustrated I wish you were hear to soothe my brow. I love you so much-- and I'm so glad for all the moments we have shared. You're a really good friend and I feel really lucky to have you. All my love..

Dedication Index

Acknowledgments

Special thanks to all the authors and those who participated in Assembly: A Social Practice Get-Together Sleepover 2014. Thanks also goes to the Portland State University Art and Social Practice MFA Program for the opportunity have The Dedication Project be apart of the programing for this event. I would also like to thank all my peers, faculty, and mentors in the Program for your support and feedback.

Thank you Nadine Edwards for being a supportive partner in my life and art practice. The things partners of artists get "wrangled" into.